The Articulate Witness

An Illustrated Guide to Testifying Confidently Under Oath

Brian K. Johnson and Marsha Hunter

CROWN KING BOOKS

Copyright © 2015 by Crown King Books
Published by Crown King Books
a division of Crown King Media, L.L.C.

Last digit in print number: 0 1 2 0 1 5 5 4 3 2

    Johnson, Brian K.
      The articulate witness : an illustrated guide to testifying confidently under oath / Brian K. Johnson and Marsha Hunter. -- First edition.
      pages cm.
      Includes bibliographical references and index.
      ISBN 978-0-9796895-2-9
      ISBN 978-1-939506-00-9
      ISBN 978-1-939506-01-6
      ISBN 978-1-939506-02-3

      1. Witnesses. 2. Communication in law. 3. Forensic oratory.   I. Hunter, Marsha. II. Title.

    K2271.J64 2014   347'.066
                    QBI14-600093

Book design and illustrations by Barbara J. Richied

Crown King Books
Santa Fe, New Mexico
crownkingbooks.com

Contents

PART THREE:

Speak Confidently

PART FOUR:

Put It All Together

To the memory of Scott Cleland.

Alphabet Adventurer, calligrapher, and court jester,
who during the syzygy of our celestial orbits taught
our eyes to hear, our ears to see, and our bellies to laugh.

Introduction

Testifying under oath is a serious conversation that may have very serious consequences. The obligation can be daunting because most people have never done it, have never been in a courtroom or arbitration conference room, and have no idea what to expect. This book gives you a plan to prepare yourself to testify calmly and well.

Every witness has a basic, simple goal: listen to each question, answer only that question, and tell the truth. Aim for that, and you can feel confident that testifying under oath needn't be some strange, intimidating experience. It is not that different from other honest, serious conversations you have had.

For a witness, the back and forth of questions and answers under oath might be compared to the game of checkers—first the lawyer's turn, then your turn, the lawyer's turn, again your turn. Listen, speak, and listen again.

Lawyers asking the questions, however, are using a more complicated strategy—more like chess than checkers. Thinking many moves ahead to reach a desired outcome, lawyers are playing to win. You cannot beat a good cross-examiner at his or her own game. Do not try. But you are not merely a pawn in that game, either.

You will benefit from understanding some of the lawyers' tactics. It helps to know what to expect. More importantly, we firmly believe that you will be most confident if you prepare to testify as your most comfortable, credible, authentic self. Reading this book will help you do that.

Lawyers are trained to exploit the rules, channel their adrenaline, think on their feet, and project their voices. They study strategies for questioning and tactics for controlling witnesses. Most witnesses, on the other hand, receive no training, get little if any practice, and don't know the rules. That seems unfair, especially since the goal of every legal proceeding is a fair and just outcome.

There are different kinds of legal proceedings and witnesses. We designed this book to be a general guide whether you are a party in a lawsuit, a "fact witness" in a civil or criminal case, a defendant being prosecuted and testifying in your own defense, or an expert witness. Our goal is to help every witness called to testify under oath in trials and arbitrations. We also describe briefly the difference between those proceedings and a deposition that may precede them.

As you use our book, keep these things in mind:

- Talk to and trust the attorney who has called you on direct examination, whether that lawyer is strictly speaking "your lawyer" (one you hired) or one calling you as a witness. If that lawyer disagrees with anything you read in this book, follow his or her advice instead. Attorneys understand the specifics of the case and we defer to them.

- Don't expect that testifying will be anything like what you watch on television or in movies. For the sake of entertainment, courtroom dramas violate the rules of court in the same way that professional wrestlers ignore the rules of athletic competition.

- Each illustrated instruction ends with a short, simple suggestion labeled **Try it.** Reading silently will only get you so far—you need to perform these exercises to fully prepare. Practice is the key to confidence. **Do it.**

- Use this book to learn what to expect and how to respond as you testify. The practical suggestions and exercises will get your body, brain, and voice ready for the challenge of answering questions honestly and credibly with greater confidence.

PART ONE:

Behave Confidently

Control how you are breathing to feel better, think better, and speak better.

As you testify under oath, you can control your feelings, thoughts, and words by controlling your breathing. Study this illustration to understand how the respiratory system works.

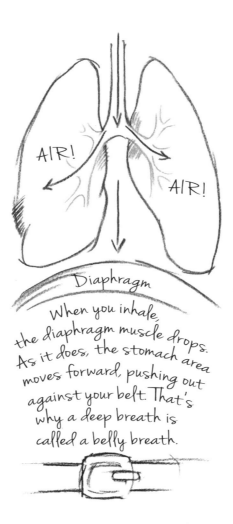

AIR!

AIR!

Diaphragm

When you inhale, the diaphragm muscle drops. As it does, the stomach area moves forward, pushing out against your belt. That's why a deep breath is called a belly breath.

Try it:

Take a deep breath. Feel that expansion deep down in your body. Push gently against your belt or waistband. Breathe low and slow.

Sit up straight to breathe easily and efficiently.

It is easier to breathe when you sit up straight. Slouching collapses your upper body against your diaphragm, making it harder to take a belly breath.

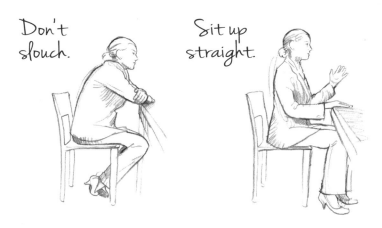

When you slouch, your head rides too far forward. Good posture is not a position you hold—"Shoulders back and chest up!"—it is a direction you feel: upward.

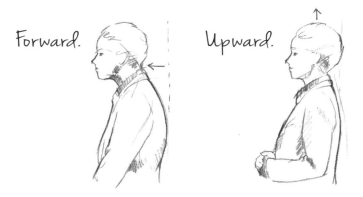

Try it:

Imagine a bungee cord is attached to the top of your skull. Feel it pull you upward gently. Don't lift or tuck your chin. Take a deep belly breath.

Use your breathing to control how you are feeling.

Breathing and feeling are connected, like the chicken and the egg. Feeling affects breathing, and breathing affects feeling. Nervous breathing is fast and shallow. Comfortable breathing is slow and deep.

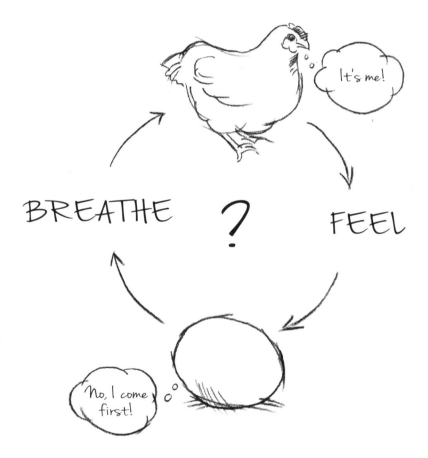

Try it:

Breathe faster and shallower than normal. How does it make you feel? Next, take slower, deeper breaths. Breathe as if you are relaxed and comfortable, and you begin to feel that way.

Breathe deeply to think clearly.

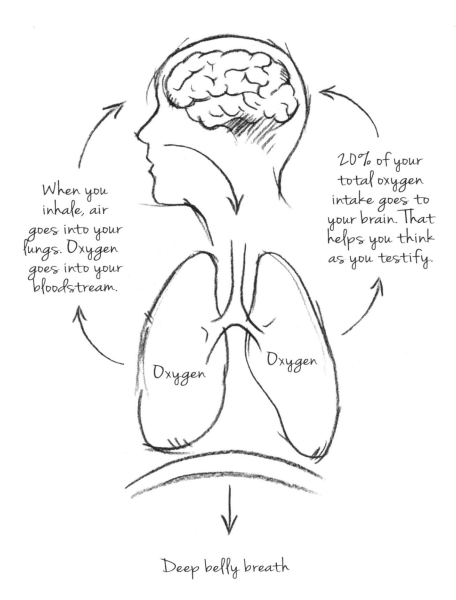

When you inhale, air goes into your lungs. Oxygen goes into your bloodstream.

20% of your total oxygen intake goes to your brain. That helps you think as you testify.

Oxygen

Oxygen

Deep belly breath

Try It:

Take a deep, slow belly breath and feel the air enter your lungs. Oxygen moves into your bloodstream and up to your brain. Breathe like this as you listen to questions.

Speak confidently and don't trail off at the end of answers.

Speak loudly enough to sound confident. Breathe deeply and have enough air to be audible at the end of the answer.

The driver who ran the red light was in the Mustang.

It happens as you run out of air.

This is another reason to breathe.

Often the point is at the end.

Be loud enough to the last word.

The driver who ran the red light was in the Mustang!

Try it:

Read aloud the sentences above, getting softer and then louder. Everyone needs to hear your answer. Be loud enough to the last word.

Relax your brow.

As you listen to questions, you may furrow your brow and tense the muscles between your eyebrows. It is easy to fix this by doing the opposite. Lift your eyebrows slightly and those muscles relax.

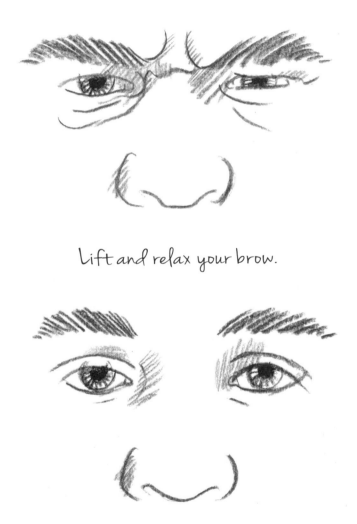

Lift and relax your brow.

Try it:

Look in a mirror or set your smartphone to "selfie." Look at your own brow. Feel the difference between tensed and relaxed. When you feel that tension, lift and relax those muscles.

Focus your eyes to focus your brain.

When you focus your eyes, it is easier to concentrate. Look at the attorney asking the questions. Listen with your eyes as well as ears. Don't let your eyes flit around.

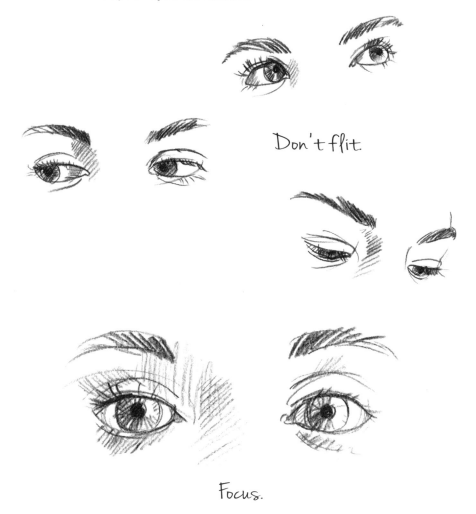

Don't flit.

Focus.

Try it:

Feel the difference. Let your eyes flit randomly from floor to ceiling to wall to ceiling to wall. Now focus your eyes on a point across the room. Take a deep, slow breath.

Testifying is both a conversation with the lawyer and a presentation to the fact finder.

In daily conversation, you answer questions to inform the questioner. When you are a witness, an attorney asks you the questions, but you answer to inform the fact finder—a judge, jury, or arbitrator. Before you testify, ask the attorney calling you on direct how often and how long you should look at, or answer directly to, the fact finder. Know your attorney's opinion on what is appropriate.

Try it:

Visit the courtroom beforehand, if you can, to see how it is arranged. Find out who sits where during the trial or arbitration.

Relax your lips when listening.

Don't tense your lips and press them tightly together. This creates a frowning, unfriendly, less believable expression. The solution, however, is not to smile; simply part your lips slightly so the mouth tension vanishes.

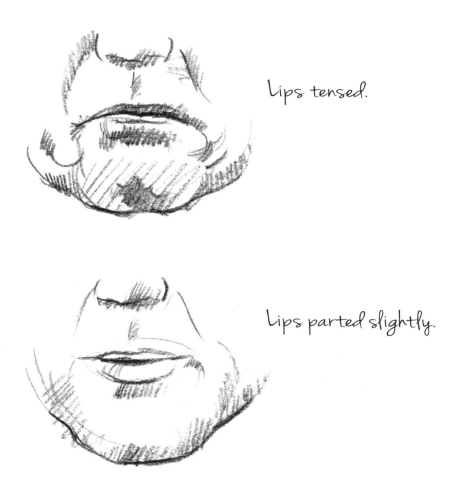

Lips tensed.

Lips parted slightly.

Try it:

Look in a mirror or set your smartphone to "selfie." Press your lips tightly together and look at the frowning result. Now part your lips slightly. Breathe easily through both your mouth and your nose.

Don't fidget with your hands while listening to questions.

Nervousness is revealed by hands. Don't wring your hands, clasp them tightly together, or lock your fingers together as if praying. Don't play with a pen, paper, jewelry, clothes, hair, paper clips, or a water glass.

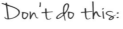

Don't do this:

Do this instead:

Rest your hands comfortably on the table.

Rest them loosely in your lap.

Try it:

Put down this book and rest your hands in your lap, one on each thigh. Now rest them one atop the other in your lap. Do the same thing at a table. Rest them on the table—separated. Rest them loosely one atop the other on the table.

Stay loose.

Natural, unconscious hand gestures are appropriate while testifying. Don't inhibit them. Don't force them, either. If they happen, let them happen.

Try it:

In daily conversation, pay attention to your own natural gestures. How big are they? Do what is natural for you as you testify.

Release your natural gestures as you speak.

Thinking, speaking, and gesturing are connected and work together.

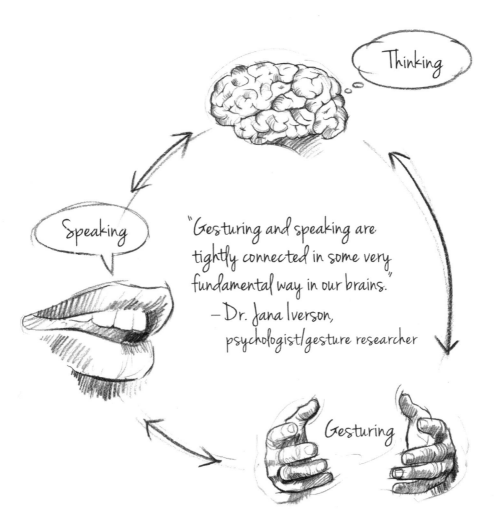

"Gesturing and speaking are tightly connected in some very fundamental way in our brains."

— Dr. Jana Iverson, psychologist/gesture researcher

Try it:

Pay attention to gestures in daily conversation. Notice how much they are connected to speaking and thinking. Trusting your natural gestures will help you think and speak.

PART TWO:

Think Confidently

Adrenaline creates a time warp in your brain.

If you feel excited or anxious as you testify, time may seem to slow down, making you acutely aware of the silence between thoughts. You may worry that too many seconds are passing while you are thinking of what to say. Adrenaline, speeding up your heart rate, has created a time warp. More beats feel like more seconds.

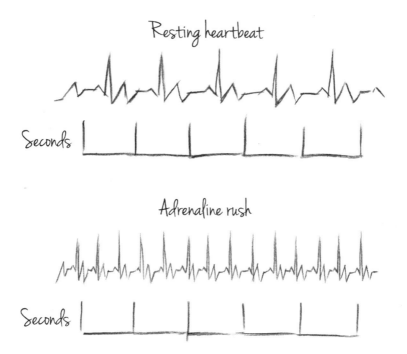

Recall a time when you felt a big adrenaline rush after being frightened or startled. People often say, "My whole life flashed in front of me!" or "Everything went into slow motion." That's the time warp.

Try it:

Practice in conversation taking a moment of silence before you speak. Breathe, think, and speak. Don't let the time warp make you rush to talk before you have considered your answer.

Think before you speak.

Before you answer the question, make sure you understand it.

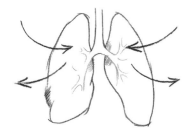

Breathe in and out as you listen.

Focus your eyes on the questioner to listen.

Question:

Be certain you understand it.

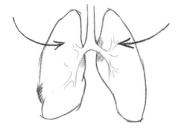

Breathe in before you speak.

Answer:

Speak out with confidence.

Try it:

Experiment in daily conversation. When someone asks you a question, think and inhale first before you answer. It only takes a second.

Know what to expect at a deposition.

Not all witnesses are deposed. If you are, the deposition will happen before the trial or arbitration.

Witness under oath

Lawyer on your side defending the deposition

Court reporter taking down every question and answer

Opposing counsel asking the questions

Video camera recording the deposition (often, not always)

Depending on the case, there may be more lawyers present as well.

Who is missing? No fact finder is present—no judge, jury, or arbitrator. What is unusual? Your attorney may object to questions. Despite no ruling on the objection, you must answer anyway.

Try it:

Talk to the lawyer who will defend your deposition so you know what to expect.

During direct examination, expect open-ended questions that use these words.

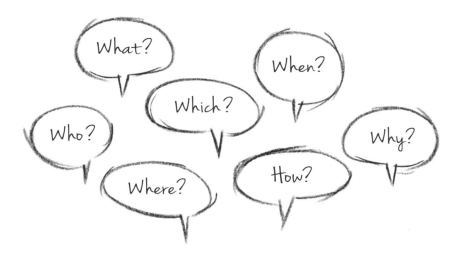

Sometimes the question is a command.

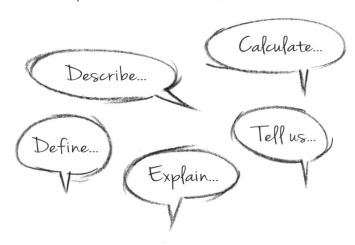

Try it:

Listen for these words in daily conversation. They get people talking. That's the purpose of these words in direct examination— to get you to tell the story in your own words.

Don't be surprised if listeners are stone-faced.

The old expression "You can't judge a book by its cover" applies to fact finders.

You can't judge listeners by their expressions.

Try it:

Notice how, in daily conversation, listeners are responsive. Heads nod. Eyebrows lift. Expressions change. Don't expect that from the fact finders. They are listening, not interacting.

Expect leading questions during cross examination.

Leading questions are designed to limit your answer to yes or no. They are often a statement turned into a question.

If the statement is . . .

You were at that meeting.

It is turned into a leading question with inflection, so it sounds like a question:

You were at that meeting?

Questioning words may be added at the end of the statement:

You were at the meeting, **correct**?
You were at the meeting, **true**?
You were at the meeting, **right**?

A questioning phrase may be added to the beginning of the statement:

Isn't it correct that you were at the meeting?
Isn't it true that you were at the meeting?
Am I right that you were at the meeting?

Be alert. If you hear an open-ended question on cross beginning with *who*, *what*, *when*, *where*, *why*, *which*, or *how*, you have the right to give a full and complete answer.

Try it:

Parents are experts at leading questions. Have you asked, or been asked, these questions? "You came home late? You didn't call, right? You didn't text, true? Isn't it correct that you promised to be home by midnight?" Be prepared for this on cross.

Have the same demeanor on cross examination as you did during direct.

One of our most experienced, savviest trial-lawyer colleagues shared his top suggestion for witnesses:

"If a witness can maintain the same demeanor on cross as on direct—posture, tone of voice, attitude—he or she is 75% of the way to success as a witness. It is somewhat harder than it sounds, but from 40+ years of watching hundreds of witnesses testify, I think this is the single most important lesson I have learned about cross examination."

Be yourself on direct and remain yourself on cross.

Don't go into a defensive crouch on cross examination.

Try it:

Practice breathing slowly and consciously, relax your facial muscles to avoid scowling, and maintain your upright posture. Relax your shoulders and neck.

Ask for a question to be repeated when you don't understand.

Don't guess or speculate about a question.

A: I didn't understand the question.
or
A: Would you please repeat the question?

Ask for clarification:

A: I don't know exactly what you mean when you say "irresponsible."

If the cross examiner says:

Q: That calls for a simple yes or no answer!

You have every right, when it is true, to respond this way:

A: I cannot answer that question with a simple yes or no.

Although the cross examiner does not want you to explain, you can try this, but don't overuse it or you will appear combative.

A: I don't think I can answer that yes or no. May I explain?

When the cross examiner says "No," he or she looks unfair.

Try it:

Say aloud the answers above several times, so that you are prepared to use them as you testify.

Don't get on the "Yes" train, and if you do, get off.

The cross examiner may ask you a series of rapid-fire questions. The "Yes" train is intended to get you answering quickly so you don't have time to think.

Q: At noon?
A: Yes.

Q: Drank one?
A: Yes

Q: Another?
A: Yes.

Q: Several.
A: Yes.

Q: Got hammered?
A: Yes.

Q: Drove drunk?
A: Yes... I mean, NO!

Try it:

In daily conversation, intentionally pause to think before you answer a question. Feel what it is like to control your own pace and take time to think.

Don't fall for this trick during cross examination.

Cross examiners want to control the witness. If you give a longer answer, the examiner may try to trick you into stopping by using this gesture.

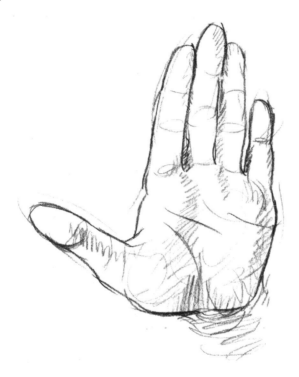

This gesture often happens after the cross examiner mistakenly asks you an open-ended question starting with *who, what, when, where, why, which,* or *how*. Give a full and complete answer. Don't be tricked into stopping by this gesture.

Try it:

To see what happens, try this "Stop" gesture on a good friend or family member. Then explain why you did it. If you fall for it once while testifying, don't fall for it twice.

If you hear an "Objection!" don't answer until the judge rules.

The opposing counsel may object to a question. Do not answer until the judge sustains or overrules the objection. There are two different possibilities:

Try it:

Practice saying aloud the request, "Please repeat the question."

Your brain thinks best in "chunks" of information.

Chunking is a word used to describe how brains process information.

Chunking is why phone numbers look like

212-555-1212 and not 2125551212

Chunking is why Social Security numbers look like

123-45-6789 and not 123456789

Chunking is why it is easier to understand

卅卅 卅卅 卅卅 卅卅 卅卅 than |||||||||||||||||||||||||

Chunking is why we give directions like this:

Go two blocks...

Turn left...

Drive one mile...

Turn right at the gate.

Brains remember and retrieve information in chunks. This simple idea can help you as you answer questions.

Your answer... can be delivered... one chunk at a time.

Q: What time did you arrive at the meeting?

A: I arrived... at the meeting... just before 9:00 a.m.

Try it:

Say aloud the driving directions above. Now say aloud the answer below it. Chunking is how your brain works to remember and speak.

PART THREE:

Speak
Confidently

Speak in phrases, not whole sentences, to control the pace.

The chunks of language are phrases. We speak in phrases or chunks when we speak together as citizens saying the Pledge of Allegiance.

I pledge allegiance... to the flag...
So that's the rhythm... I can use...

of the United States of America.
to control the pace of my answers.

Try it:

Say aloud the first sentence of the Pledge in three distinct phrases. Now say the instruction below it using that same rhythm.

Think in silence—momentarily—between phrases and sentences.

To answer questions truthfully and accurately, you need time to think as you speak. When you speak in phrases, and think in silence between those phrases, you maintain control.

The secret *(Silence)* to thinking clearly *(Silence)*

and speaking confidently *(Silence)* as you

answer each question *(Silence)* is to say your

answer in chunks, *(Silence)* a phrase at a time.

Try It:

Say aloud, a phrase at a time, the sentence above. Once you feel that rhythm, finish this thought in phrases: The last time . . . I took a vacation . . . I went . . .

A descending vocal pattern makes you sound confident.

You have used this pattern unconsciously in conversation many times. It's called "walking down the steps."

Say aloud the last phrase of the Pledge of Allegiance and listen to the sound and direction of your own voice:

...with liberty and justice for all.

You "walked down the steps" to a lower pitch level.

Say these examples aloud:

May The Force be with you.

May the wind be at your back.

Use your common sense.

That is not true.

I cannot recall.

I completely disagree.

Try it:

Experiment with this descending vocal pattern in your daily conversation. It makes you sound sure of yourself.

Avoid the vocal pattern called "uptalk" that sounds like a question.

There is a common habit of inflection that makes statements sound like questions. Beware of this "uptalk" or "uptick" at the ends of phrases and sentences.

Lots of people
in daily conversation
end their phrases
and their sentences
with a vocal pattern that rises up?

You would never say:

May The Force be with you?
May the wind be at your back?

You would say:

May
—— The Force be with you.

May
the wind be at your back.

Try it:

Say aloud the sentences above and hear your voice rising or falling as the illustrations suggest.

Emphasize important words.

When you emphasize different words, you get a different meaning. Look at how the shifting emphasis on this answer makes it mean different things:

He told me to shred those documents.

He **told** me to shred those documents.

He told **me** to shred those documents.

He told me to **shred** those documents.

He told me to shred **those** documents.

He told me to shred those **documents**.

When several words are emphasized, it sounds even more important:

He told **me** to **shred** those **documents**.

Try it:

Read aloud the statements above and emphasize the highlighted word in each one. Notice how the meaning changes. Say the sentence with several words highlighted and hear how it sounds more important.

Emphatic gestures and emphatic words work together.

The main reason to trust your natural gestures is that gestures will make you speak more energetically, confidently, and emphatically.

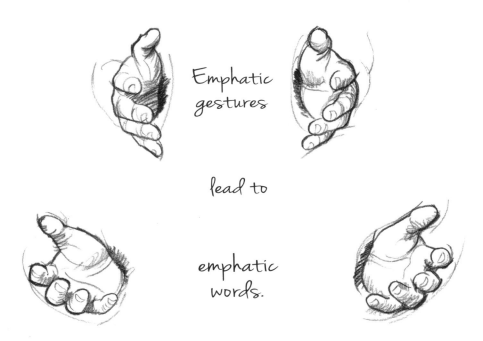

Emphatic gestures

lead to

emphatic words.

Try it:

Say aloud the caption above while doing the gesture in the illustration.

Speak loudly enough to be heard by everyone all the time.

If the examiner is speaking in a loud, confident voice, and you are not, you sound uncertain and insecure.

Q: Who did you speak with after the incident?
A: I talked with my supervisor.

Q: Where did that conversation take place?
A: In his office.

Match the volume and sound more certain on direct:

Q: Who did you speak with after the incident?
A: I talked with my supervisor.

Q: Where did that conversation take place?
A: In his office.

Do the same on cross. Don't be too soft:

Q: You spoke with your supervisor after the incident, true?

A: Yes.

Q: You were in his office, correct?

A: Yes.

Match the volume and sound confident:

Q: You spoke with your supervisor after the incident, true?

A: Yes.

Q: You were in his office, correct?

A: Yes.

There are two instances when you do not want to match the lawyer's volume: (1) If a lawyer is speaking too softly, you should continue to speak loudly enough to be heard. (2) If the cross examiner starts to yell at you, do not yell back. Keep your cool and speak softer to control your emotions.

Q: ARE YOU TELLING THIS JURY YOU NEVER READ THAT EMAIL!!?

A: That is correct. I did not.

Try it:

Read all these answers aloud with confidence.

A good cross examiner can make you eat your own words, and that can be tough to swallow.

Sometimes the questioner knows your answers better than you do. You do not want to hear this question during cross:

You gave a different answer under oath the last time, didn't you?

I can't remember exactly what I said before!

Gulp!

Imagine you are a witness in a dispute over a toxic spill. During your *deposition* you answered with these words:

Q: Why didn't you report the spill immediately?

A: I hoped we could fix the leak.

During *direct examination* at trial you innocently use different words:

Q: Describe your response to discovering the spill.

A: I was concerned about the leak, but I was sure we could fix it.

A good cross examiner can leap on that slight change and make you squirm. Under oath you said two different things. Both can't be true, so you can't be trusted.

Try it:

Ask the attorney calling you on direct what you must read and review to be ready for your testimony. While you prepare, don't just read silently; read key portions out loud to get some muscle memory about what you said months or even years before. Don't memorize those passages, but say the key words and phrases of your previous answers.

PART FOUR:

Put It All Together

Behave
Confidently

Put it all
together

Think
Confidently

Speak
Confidently

Confident actions lead to increased confidence.

Recall that old question about the chicken, the egg, and which comes first. We conclude with one last riddle. Which comes first, your confidence or your actions? In other words, do you feel confident first, and then act that way? Or do you behave confidently, and those actions make you feel confident?

According to cutting-edge research by Dr. Richard E. Petty, Distinguished University Professor of Psychology at Ohio State University, the answer can be summed up this simply:

Confident actions can boost your confidence.

Try it:

Actions are easier to control than feelings. So practice the actions suggested in this book. Review the few final sentences at the bottom of each page. Don't just read it, do it. Identify those actions you find most helpful. Breathing, gesturing, focusing, pausing, speaking in phrases, emphasizing, and "walking down the steps"—these are all actions. The more you do them, the more you will feel confident as you testify under oath.

Common Advice for Testifying

We've combed through books, brochures, and websites about witness preparation and compiled the collective wisdom of judges, lawyers, and court administrators.

Plan ahead:

- Find out where the courthouse or deposition room is located, how to get there, and where to park.

- Visit the courtroom in advance if you can. Courts are public places, so you may visit.

- Arrange to get off work in advance of testifying.

- Wear neat, tidy clothes. Ask the attorney calling you on direct for further advice about appropriate courtroom attire.

- Before testifying, review any statements you have already given.

- Leave in plenty of time so you are not rushing to get there at the last minute.

- Be aware that courthouse security may not allow you to bring your cell phone into court.

- Bring something to do or read while you wait.

- Especially if you are victim of a crime or domestic violence, be prepared to see people in the courtroom whose presence may be upsetting to you.

Once you arrive:

- Sit down and calm down once you arrive.

- Do not talk about your testimony with other witnesses.

- Know the jury is watching you from the moment you are called and enter the courtroom.

- Keep breathing consciously.

- Do not chew gum.

While under oath:

- Be attentive and alert.

- Be polite, thoughtful, sincere, and honest.

- When speaking to the judge, address her or him as "Your Honor."

- Speak loudly enough for everyone to hear. Microphones may be present to record the trial, not to amplify your voice.

- Answer out loud, not with a nod or shake of your head.

- Don't start to answer until the attorney finishes each question. Pause to think first.

- Never guess at an answer.

- Avoid the phrases "I think . . ." "I guess . . ." "In my opinion . . ." "If I remember correctly . . ." If you are sure about something, say so. If not, say "I'm not sure" or "I don't remember."

- Answer the question and stop. Do not volunteer additional information.

- Do not roll your eyes at questions you think are irrelevant, dumb, or silly.

- Avoid joking and wisecracks.

- Do not lose your temper. Keep your cool.

- Don't take questions personally or become upset by an attorney's questions.

- Beware of questions involving distance and time, and try not to estimate numbers you are not sure of.

- Expect to be questioned by attorneys for both sides.

- Do not answer if you hear the word "Objection!" Wait for the judge to rule.

- Stop immediately when the judge interrupts you.

Remember:

The outcome of the trial is not your responsibility. You are testifying to tell the fact finders the evidence you know. It is the responsibility of the fact finders to make a decision based on which facts they find most persuasive.

Acknowledgments

While creating this book, we were fortunate to have the assistance of our generous and gifted colleagues—judges, trial lawyers, and law professors—who were kind enough to offer us feedback about this unusual manuscript.

We gratefully thank (in alphabetical order): Hon. Jane M. Beckering, Luke L. Dauchot, Mary Pat Dooley, John C. Goodchild III, Professor Zelda Harris, Christopher Houk, Stuart S. Jorgensen, Steven D. McCormick, Terre Rushton, and Raymond M. White. This book was much improved by their insightful wisdom.

Special thanks to our illustrator, Barbara J. Richied, whose boundless creativity and unflagging efficiency has made her an invaluable part of all our work.

To our publisher, Amanda Fessler at Crown King Books, we have no greater thanks than this: We simply can't imagine what we would do without you.

Thanks to all who made this book better.

About the Authors

Brian K. Johnson and **Marsha Hunter** are communication consultants who train attorneys to speak confidently and persuasively in all settings. They are principals in Johnson & Hunter, Inc. (johnson-hunter.com), with legal clients in the United States, Canada, Australia, and Europe.

Johnson and Hunter are co-authors of *The Articulate Advocate: New Techniques of Persuasion for Trial Lawyers* (2009), *The Articulate Attorney: Public Speaking for Lawyers* (2010; second edition 2013), and *The Articulate Witness: An Illustrated Guide to Testifying Confidently Under Oath* (2015). Find more information at crownkingbooks.com.

Brian K. Johnson   Marsha Hunter

About the Illustrator

Barbara J. Richied is a graphic designer and illustrator living in Minneapolis, Minnesota. She has designed for print, video, and the web. Her client list includes 3M, St. Jude Medical, Best Buy, and Aveda.

Notes and Questions for My Lawyer